ODE *to a* MOTHER TREE

Written by
Jamie Bastedo

Illustrated by
James Savage

FITZHENRY & WHITESIDE

Toronto 2026

Published in Canada by Fitzhenry & Whiteside
416 Moore Avenue, Unit 304, Toronto, ON, M4G 1C9

ONTARIO ARTS COUNCIL
CONSEIL DES ARTS DE L'ONTARIO
an Ontario government agency
un organisme du gouvernement de l'Ontario

Canada Council for the Arts
Conseil des arts du Canada

Fitzhenry and Whiteside acknowledges with thanks the Canada Council for the Arts and the Ontario Arts Council for their support of our publishing program. We acknowledge the financial support of the Government of Canada through the Canada Book Fund (CBF) for our publishing activities.

Author photo: Paul Bastedo
Illustrator photo: Michael Savage
Cover designed by Jordan Lunn
Book composed by Karl Hunt
Printed in China

Library and Archives Canada Cataloguing in Publication
Title: Ode to a mother tree / written by Jamie Bastedo;
illustrated by James Savage.
Names: Bastedo, Jamie, 1955- author.
Description: Includes bibliographical references.
Identifiers: Canadiana 20250320193 | ISBN 9781554556922 (softcover)
Subjects: LCGFT: Poetry.
Classification: LCC PS8553.A82418 O34 2026 | DDC C811/.54—dc23

ISBN (softcover) 978-1-55455-692-2

www.fitzhenry.ca

Praise for *ODE TO A MOTHER TREE*

"I love the story's premise and [Bastedo's] commitment to the Haiku form for telling it . . . Full of playful sounds and fresh imagery . . . Timely and necessary . . . Accessible to a wide range of readers . . . This is the next generation of *The Giving Tree*, by Shel Silverstein, which was radical in showing the importance of trees in our world."

—Rayya Liebich, Award-winning poet,
Poet-in-residence for ArtStarts BC

"[Bastedo's] Haiku poems are wonderfully simple and echo the great masters of the Haiku form . . . A great, elemental vision . . . Very moving and mesmerizing . . . Gave me goosebumps. Beautiful!"

—Ross Breithaupt, Author of *Midland* and
Contributor to *The Globe and Mail*

"What a beautiful vision and so skillfully manifested! The story invites us to sit, relax, and listen, as if gathered around a campfire in an old-growth forest . . . Marvellous to intimately witness the growth of one tree, and the changes around it, over a millennium."

—Stuart McKinnon, Sufi teacher and musician

"Skillfully evokes a profound empathy and concern for old-growth trees . . . The whole storyline, leading to a conservation objective, is both powerful and creative."

—John Theberge, Biologist and Author of *Wolf Country*

"I found the story both clever and profound and, I admit, I even teared up a couple of times . . . I thought Bastedo's use of the Haiku form both deft and appropriate as a story-telling vehicle for this particular work. Haiku can sometimes feel stilted and forced, but Bastedo's flowed naturally."

—Hayden Trenholm, Playwright, publisher, and
award-winning science fiction author

"When I first read the description I thought, 'How the heck is Bastedo going to hold my interest about a tree for the length of a book?' And he did just that . . . The choice of Haiku for this project really works. I definitely felt the tautness of the story and could see everything in a short time, even though we're moving through such a great span of years . . . The story's felt sense of time is part of the beauty of this work, and reminds readers of their own planetary connections . . . A very marketable read!

—Sonnet L'Abbé, Poet, Vancouver Island University professor, CBC Artist-in-Motion

PRAISE FOR BASTEDO'S WRITING

"An engaging storyteller who combines the knowledge of a naturalist with the eye of an artist and the curiosity of a child."

—Arctic

"The author situates himself in the landscape with passion, immediacy and refreshingly sharp powers of observation."

—Canadian Geographic

"A masterful blend of clever plot, commentary on current social and environmental challenges, and characters as real as the problems they face."

—Books in Canada

"Today, just for today,
I need to be you—
Red Cedar, let me be you."

—Shirley Martin, "Trading Places" in *Worth More Standing*

"Consider the other kingdoms.
The trees, for example . . . with their infallible sense
of what their lives are meant to be."

—Mary Oliver, *The Truro Bear and Other Adventures*

"Great cedar trees, with clear, true grain,
are becoming difficult to find as more of them
succumb to the logger's saw, yet there is no other tree that
can provide so generously, so totally and so beautifully."

—Hilary Stewart, *Cedar*

"Each time I work with cedar
there is a lesson or learning experience.
Cedar is a gift that requires gratitude, humility, and patience.
Cedar's beauty holds light, and like human skin,
it has many vital layers within."

—Patti Bailey, Sinixt weaver of traditional baskets,
The Geography of Memory

"If you don't believe there's a god, then think about this tree.
Watch how a tree matures from a very small seed
to become very large and complex.
This is the work of the Creator."

—Madeleine Paul Desautel, Sinixt Elder,
The Geography of Memory

For my grandchildren.
May they learn to love, protect,
And whisper to trees.

—J.B.

For Sam.

—J.S.

ODE:

A lyrical poem that praises or pays tribute to a specific idea, person, place, or element of nature.

This is the story
Of one tree. Well, two, really.
Two cedar sisters.

Come and sit with me.
You'll see . . .

Look! A tiny seed,
Floating through a smoke-streaked sky.
Woodpecker watches.

Buried in fresh ash,
Safe in a scorched stump, our seed
Sleeps off its long flight.

Gravity, darkness,
And a feather-touch of rain,
Stir the small seed's heart.

The scent of sunbeams!
The seed swells, cracks, pops, unlocks,
Waking its secrets.

Fierce force of nature,
It sends roots down, sends shoots up,
Gripped by one wild wish:

Grow!

Bursting through blackness
One green spear stabs at the sun,
Feasting on photons.

It gulps down sunlight,
Like baby's first slurps of milk.
How magic is *that?*

There! Another shoot
Pops out of the ash, it too,
Hungry for sunlight.

One Earth-twirl around
Our life-showering sun. Hey,
Two seedling sisters!

Two slight light-beings,
All green fuzz and tender bark,
Quietly helpless.

They feel beetle feet,
Gnawing mice, crushing bear paws,
Wonderment of wind.

They rise together,
Brushing branches, dreaming of
The future forest.

Craving connection,
They join roots, clinging, coiling,
Weaving endless braids.

So many seedlings,
Greening the dead dry ash-field,
Shouting *YES!* to life.

But . . .

So many seedlings,
Swallowed by the four-leggeds.
Who will be the next?

Amber eyes flare-stare
From the unburned forest edge,
Hungry for elk meat.

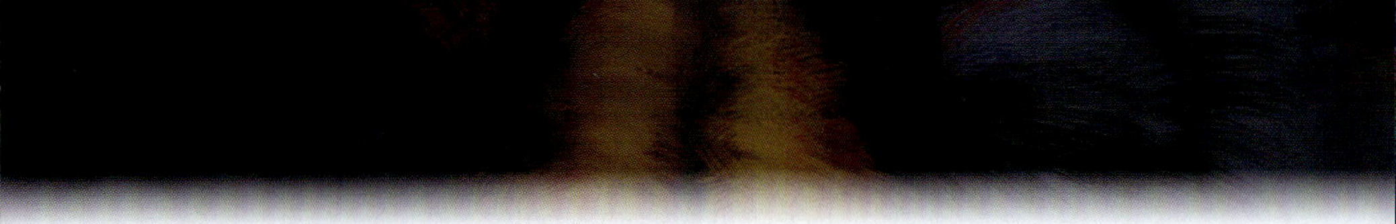

Wolf pack leap-lunges,
Keen elk stops browsing, breathing—
Then runs for its life!

If we could but hear,
The frightened gasps of seedlings,
Now, sighs of relief.

Five Earth-twirls around
Our mother star sun. Behold,
How our sisters grow!

But, they don't look good.
Weak, hungry, wilted by thirst,
Marooned, stump-stranded.

Then, from deep below,
Smoochy clicks, crackles, and pops.
They grope for the ground.

A new world opens!
Soft, woolly threads clasp their roots,
Mingling . . . melding . . . meshed.

Connections fan out,
Like wheels of pitch-forked lightning,
Sucking secret strength.

Soon . . .

Help floods in along
Fungi flumes, streaming life to
Our stranded sisters.

Web-woven below,
Our saplings stand tall and lift
Their birdlike branches.

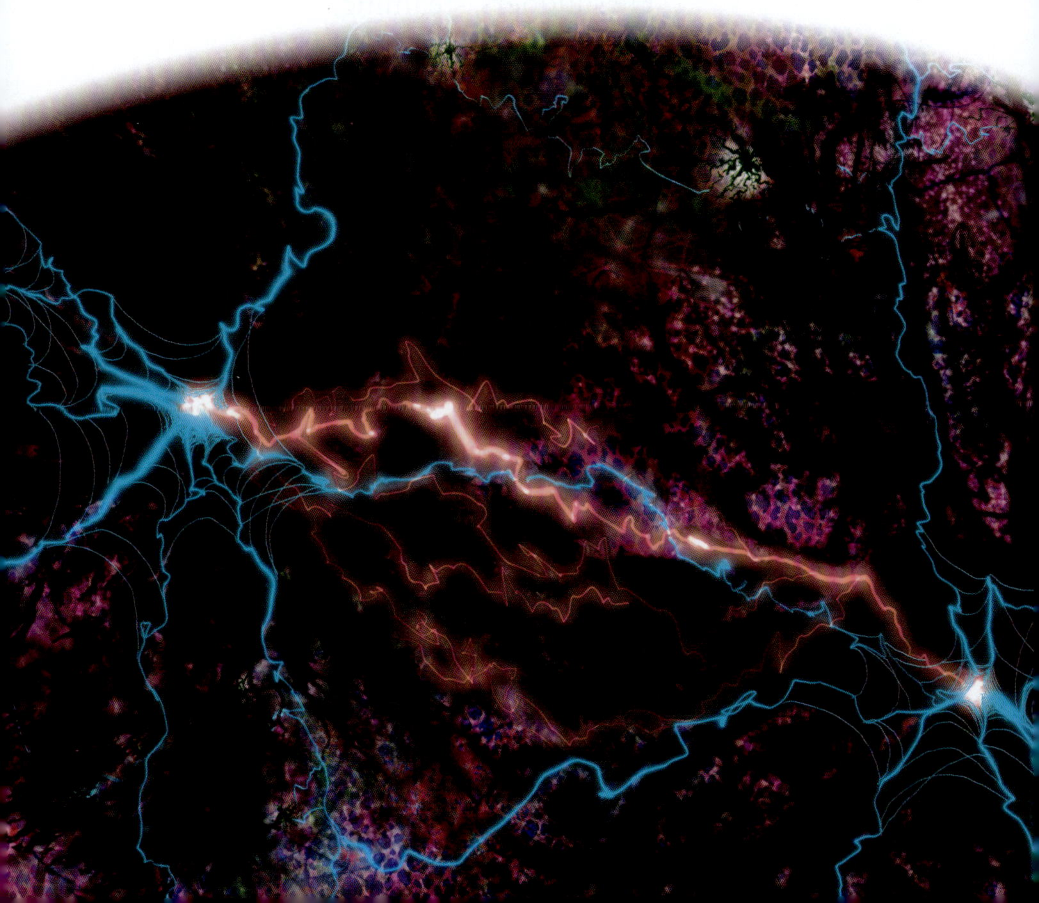

Now ten Earth-twirls old,
Fledgling forest holds its breath.
Our two trees tremble.

Behind that willow . . .
Something . . . Something huffs. Blood boils.
Look out! A mad moose!

Mad, with mating fire,
Aching for something to rub his
Prickling antlers on.

He shudders, steaming,
Raging to ram anything
That gets in his way.

Flaming eyes, flashing hooves,
He charges the big sapling.
She bends and she breaks.

He stomps and rips and
Tears at her tender branches,
Spills her sap like blood.

A gummy ooze glues
Open wounds shut, lets loose a
Perfumed plea for *HELP!*

Stress message received.
In far-off unburned forests,
Mother trees listen.

Their riot of roots
Swaps sweets and plant medicines.
Mother trees answer.

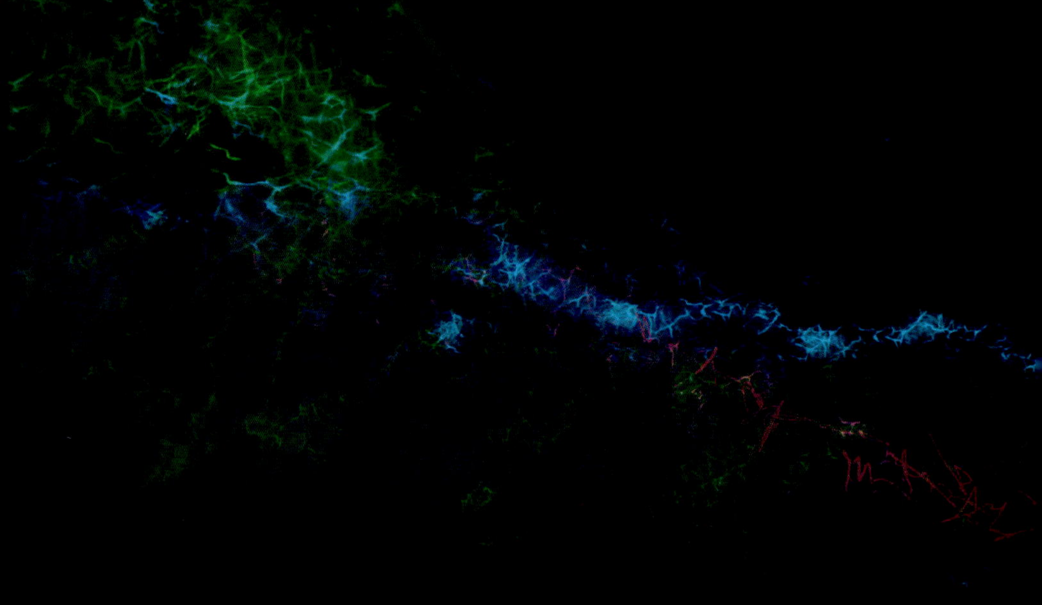

Poor moose-mashed sapling
Feels warm tickles in her roots,
Strength in hunchbacked boughs.

Oh, to grow older,
With a tower trunk, like those
Gentle, giant moms!

Sixteen hushed spins past
Planets and comets and dust,
Our two trees erupt.

Roots split, spread, touch, taste,
Fresh frail branches bump and slump.
Awkward teenage trees.

Gangly-trunked sisters
Caught in a growth spurt, puzzling
Their path to the sky.

Now fifty years old
Two trees—call them adults—
With still much to learn.

The First People come,
Pulled by sleeping powers in
The taller sister.

More than deep shared breaths,
Something passes between them,
From tree . . . humans . . . tree.

Tucked in her heartwood,
A quick twinkling-inkling of
The tree she can be.

On stone, in rust-red,
For generations to see,
They paint a promise.

Sway-swishing branches,
Both sisters watch and wonder,
In their own tree way.

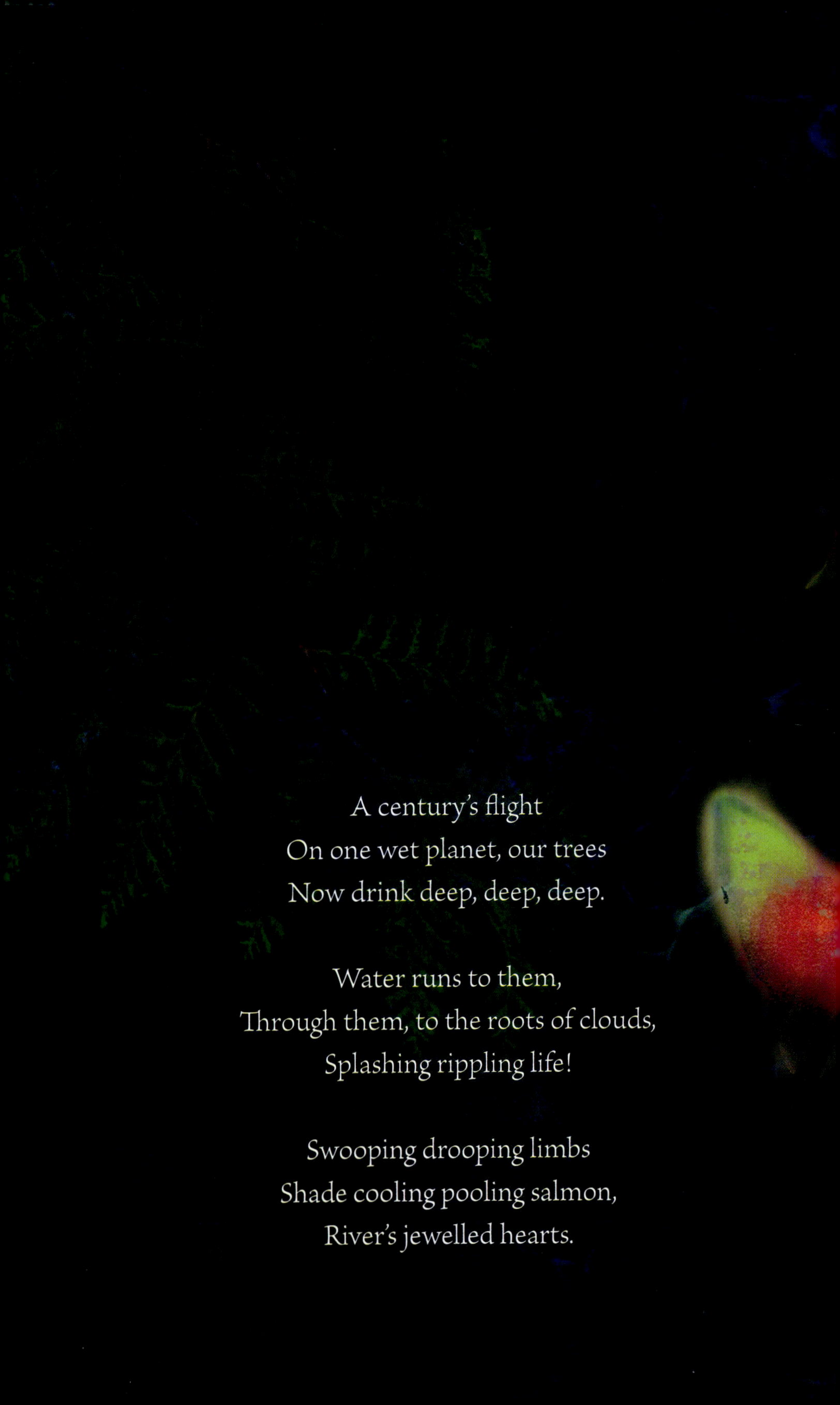

A century's flight
On one wet planet, our trees
Now drink deep, deep, deep.

Water runs to them,
Through them, to the roots of clouds,
Splashing rippling life!

Swooping drooping limbs
Shade cooling pooling salmon,
River's jewelled hearts.

First People spear them,
Bears ambush them, pounce on them.
Birds scoop fatty eggs.

Salmon give and give!
Cast-off fish heads, guts, bones, feed
Bugs, slugs, even trees.

Late winter cold snap
Relaxes. Snow crystals too,
Dangerously so.

Upslope from our trees,
With a loud *wumpf* and a *woosh*,
Old snow load explodes.

The mountain lets go,
Sneezing its snow. She stoops for
Her smaller sister.

White wall of thunder
Twists her trunk, butchers branches,
But the small one's safe.

Warm Spring wind reveals
Tangled mangled mess—smash-up
From the avalanche.

Sound of meltwater.
Careful footprints in soiled snow,
Hopping with snow fleas.

A splinter-stripped stump
Gives scant cover for hunter,
His young heart pounding.

Aims for elk. Misses.
Chiseled quartzite spearpoint stabs
Big tree's buckled trunk.

Scarred for life, she wraps
Her wounds with tight, tough wood, now
Stronger than ever.

More sweeping sun spins,
Two tall sisters now stout enough
To block wind, block rain.

Drawn by their shelter,
On a cold, wet autumn night,
First People come back.

Drawn by healing and
New life in this fire-scarred land,
They bring many gifts.

Gifts for our sisters:
Eagle feathers, arrowheads,
Pink salmon-shaped rocks.

They bring their tree songs,
Happy, hopeful songs, cheering
The trees they can be.

Fat mother spider
Looks on, tapping all eight feet.
Joy in the forest!

After five hundred
Flights round our solar system,
Big sister tops all.

Her highest branches
Breach the forest ceiling like
Gothic candlesticks,

Lit by daybreak's match,
Pinnacles of nature's reach,
Magnets for eagles.

The *thump* of salmon,
Dropped from eagle mother's claws,
Thrills the tall tree's crown,

Bent and busted by
A moose so long, long ago,
Now an eagle nursery.

Eight hundred Earth-twirls.
Remember those ashy wastes?
Just look what happened.

An old-growth forest!
From its dark webbed wonderworld,
To its dazzling dome,

Home to begging owls,
And crimson-crowned woodpeckers,
Yowling, howling wolves.

Lean in, to tree skin.
You'll hear gurgling-swirgling, a
Gushing give-and-take.

Lavish, lichen-draped,
Sporting sleeves of moss, these trees
Pulse with plush, lush life.

First People return,
Down generations-long trail,
To two jumbo trees.

They come to bury
One of their own, an elder,
A tree whisperer.

They choose the big one,
By the rust-red rock painting.
Humbly ask for bark,

Peel off supple strips,
Weave a grandma-sized cradle
To hold their loved one,

Sling her to a bough,
Wait for her body to free
Its last sparks of life.

In the cedar's shade,
By the cool salmon stream's banks,
They gently plant her.

Curled like a fetus,
She faces downstream, looking
East to greet the sun.

Old songs and drumming
Rest-nestle her into veiled
Under wonderworld.

Silently, the stream
Washes her flesh into tides
To merge with the sea.

Silently, our tree
Gathers her bones into roots,
Breathes her into clouds.

The settlers arrive.
Strangers hunt for silver, gold,
And towers of wood.

Pioneer loggers,
So hungry for wood, eyeball
The straighter sister.

Wood to build farms, towns,
Train tracks and telegraph poles.
Masts for tall ships.

We settlers need wood,
Always have, always will. But
Pray, spare the ancients.

Baffling vibrations,
Slashing-gashing, shaking-quaking.
Does a tree feel fear?

They slice that straight one.
Her half-sawn stump splits open
With a cannon *CRACK!*

She tips, teeters, rakes
The sky, slams her bent sister,
Clip-strips her branches.

They drop her, drag her,
Leave crooked one more damaged,
Both outside and in.

Tree-time drip-slips on.
Broken heartwood slowly heals.
Lone tree grows in peace.

Nine hundred Earth-twirls:
Chunky trunk, tree-sized branches,
Underworld wizard.

From her farthest roots,
To her highest feathered fronds,
She tastes everything:

Soil, sky, and sunshine,
Rain, snow, the flavour of wind,
Of running water,

A troubled tree's scent,
The wishes of a warbler,
And yes, humans too.

Nothing slips past her,
She learns all their languages,
Sipping the forest.

Our grand old cedar,
A giant among giants,
And *still* she rises!

Swirls of bare branches
Part like a dress, revealing
Old scars and new strength.

Imprints of moose, snow,
Her toppling sister. Gashes
And gifts from humans.

Floating fleck of life,
Ash-cradled forest maker,
Now full-blown mother.

Under her shelter,
A green tide of little ones
Waiting to become.

Where is the water?
The sky so dry, the land parched.
The young ones wither.

She pushes and pulls,
Shunts water from her deep, wide
Underground bloodstream.

Calls her fungi friends,
Whose spongy sprigs hug their roots,
And her children drink.

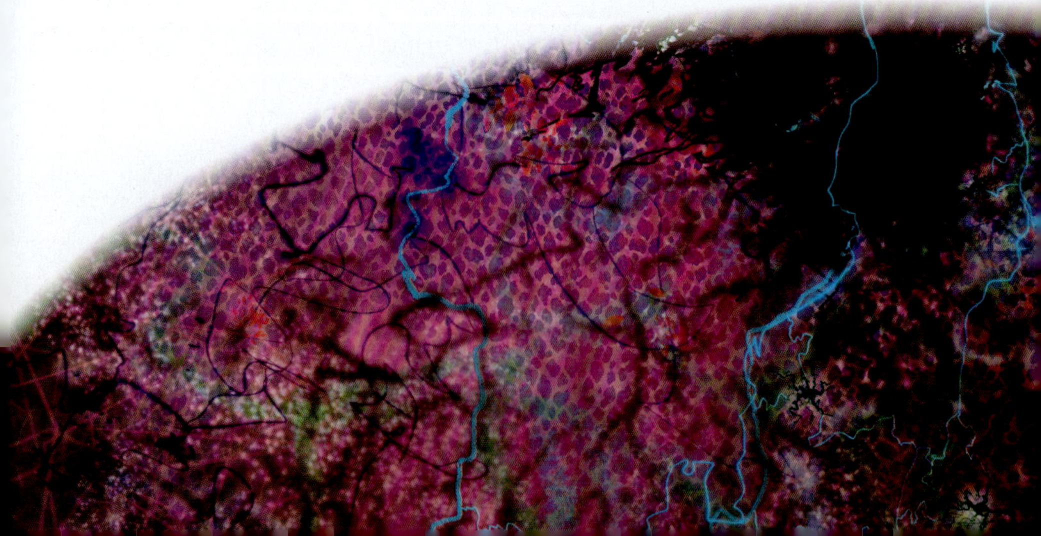

Grown from tiny seeds,
Dropped from her crown, by squirrels,
Birds, the wind and rain.

Her children, at first
So flimsy and frail, might too
Be mothers like her.

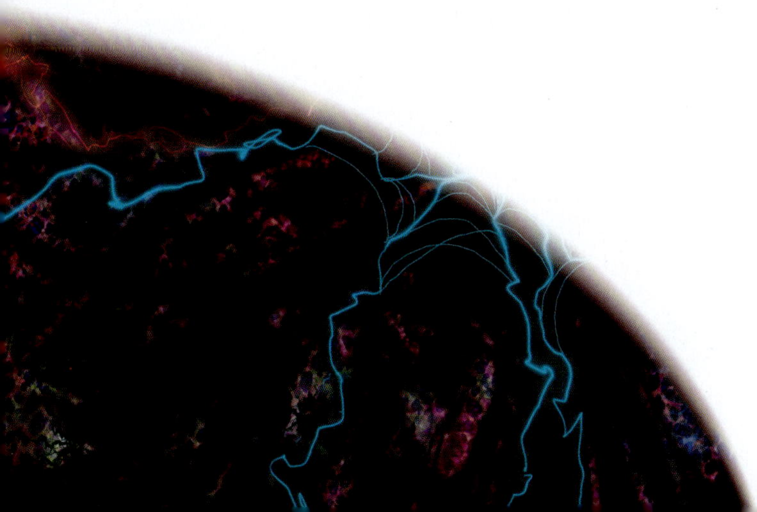

First People come back,
Led by a tall teen, Richard,
Searching for something.

They build a small fire,
Speak softly, pass food, Richard
Always looking up.

Up at that giant,
Listening for he-knows-not-what.
That's what they told him.

You listen and wait,
Don't take your eyes off that tree.
They leave him. Alone.

Night dips to freezing.
He wakes shivering, sore, starved.
Is the tree bigger?

Wraps in thin blankets,
Paces round and round the trunk,
Each spin, five minutes.

Palms the fissured bark,
Shoves his face in it, hugs it.
What does this tree feel?

Stomach still grumbling,
He chucks stones in the creek.
Spooked wood duck blasts off.

He builds a lean-to
At the feet of the giant,
Makes a moss mattress.

Streams of cedar dreams.
Wakes to hooting great horned owl,
Runs out under stars.

Sleek owl's silhouette
Streaks across the Milky Way.
Tears fill Richard's eyes.

Tree-time slows, then stops.
She tastes the air around him,
Sensing readiness.

She dives deep, deeper,
Milks wealth of webbed wonderworld
Into her roots, trunk.

She strains for the stars,
Gathers their wild, wondrous light
Into her branches.

She opens to this
Curious boy who shares her
Flowing, glowing life.

Rooted forever,
Where her seed fell, she shimmers,
Lighting up the world.

Richard unearths it,
What he was looking for, what
We must never lose.

He finds it inside,
That place where we all can see
Nature's magic light.

One thousand Earth-twirls.
A new kind of visitor
Exploring our tree.

A spirit squirrel?
No, it's a girl, climbing her,
Up and up and up.

She is Sienna,
Old-growth forest defender.
She's on a mission.

Helpers rope supplies.
Sienna pulls, struggles, and sweats.
Yells down, "Bring it on!"

Up comes all she'll need
To stay for weeks, maybe months.
Whatever it takes.

She pulls up the ropes.
Helpers fling her air hugs,
Then leave her. Alone.

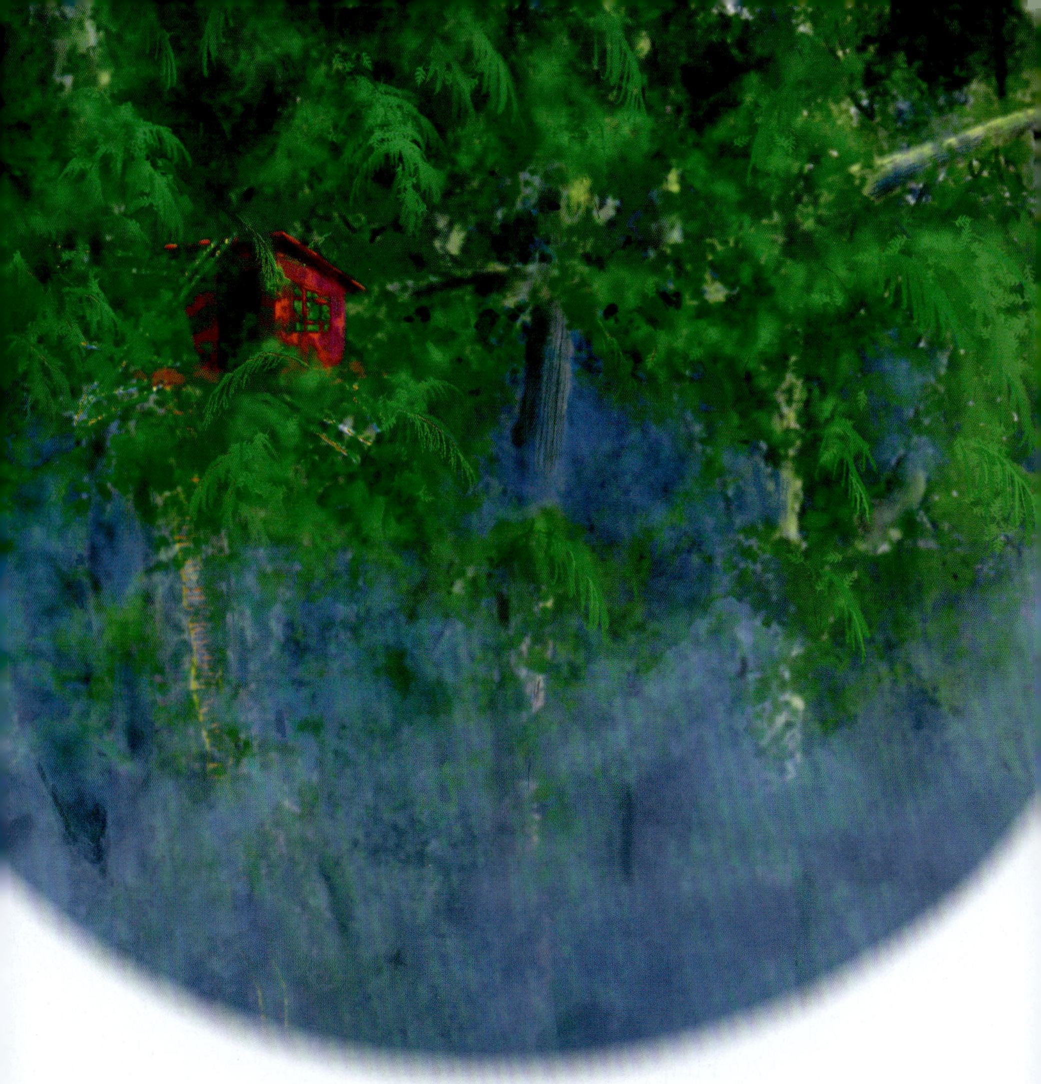

She builds a treehouse
On the moose branch. Guards the giant
With her love songs.

Wonderful mother,
I will live in your branches
Until you are safe,
Until you are safe.

Heart of the forest,
I will sing of your beauty
Until you are safe,
Until you are safe.

Magnificent tree,
I will fight to protect you
Until you are safe,
Until you are safe.

Words fall away but
Her songs pour on, spill from her
Thrumming-humming heart.

The cloud-curled forest
Inhales her sweet-scented songs
Through numberless lungs.

From her sky-high perch
She watches the slow advance,
Hears its deadly dance.

The forest echoes
To the razor drumbeat of
Helicopter blades.

Sunrise to sunset,
Distant chainsaws rip the air,
Whining for more wood.

Thin ribbons of trees,
Sway weirdly, then disappear,
Bulldozed off the Earth.

Muck road steers closer,
Vanguard of the invading
Plague of industry.

All this spurs her on
To give voice to the voiceless
Open to attack.

Many helpers come,
Lured by her songs, and love for
Wild green precious life.

They sing in one voice.
They join hands and block the road.
They chain to our tree.

Many police come.
They replace chains with handcuffs.
They take them away.

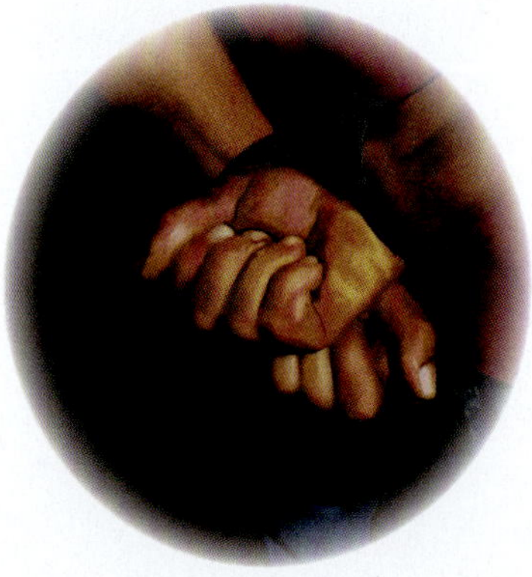

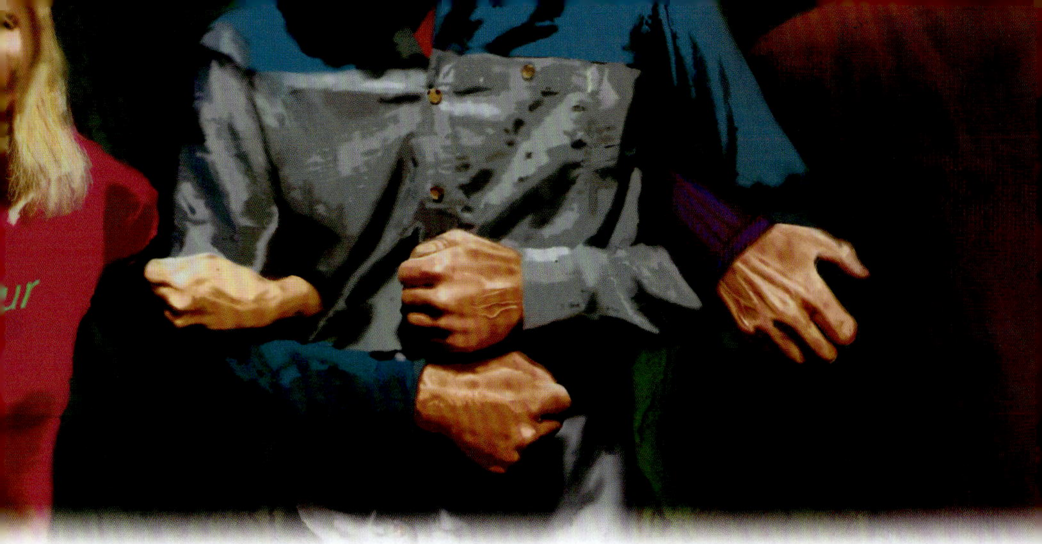

But Sienna stays.
"Come down!" shouts the Bossman. "Now!
It's not safe up there."

"Trust me, I'm quite safe.
We seriously should talk.
Till then, I'm staying."

A long pregnant pause . . .
"Fine. Let me get back to you."
She smiles. "Roger that."

So . . . our tree is spared,
As long as she can hold on,
Way up there, singing.

Bare feet are the best,
To climb, to connect, to feel
Her beloved tree.

Even in winter?
Sienna tried. Froze her feet.
Almost lost a toe.

Lip-splitting laughter!
Oh, sugar-frosted forest!
So go her good days.

White-knuckle snowstorms.
Lonely starless nights. Dead phone.
So go her bad days.

Tentacles of cold
Grab hold of her promise, try
To squeeze it to death.

Where are her helpers
Who bring food, fuel, and news from
Her long-ago world?

Misery kicks in.
She shouts to the brittle dawn,
"Enough! Can't do this!"

Heavy huffing. "*What?*"
Sound of moose plodding through snow.
No . . . Wait a minute . . .

The crunch of snowshoes!
Sienna jumps up, yells down,
"I *so* love you guys!"

Gifts roped on, she pulls.
A new sleeping bag. Fat socks.
Chocolatey toffees!

A solar panel
To charge her phone, her radio.
Crazy bright headlamps.

A special surprise
From a First Peoples' family:
A fine elk-hide drum.

More fresh journals to
Catch her heart-art, inspired by
Empire of cedars.

Sienna's staying.

Her body defrosts.
Still, her big bad dream haunts her:
A huge . . . bleeding . . . stump.

And there she is, on
That sorry stump, fetal-curled,
Weeping and weeping.

The dream stokes her fire
To give this tree voice, praise its
More-than-human world.

Industry's march halts
For winter, surrendering
To supreme silence.

The trees stop growing,
But not this girl, flourishing
On silence and hope.

A deathless hope that,
In another thousand years,
Trees like these still thrive.

One mild, misty day,
Our tree stirs, the silence breaks.
The Bossman comes back.

"Hey, you've made your point!
It's okay to come down now.
We can save your tree."

"I don't think so, Sir.
"Not until you prove she's safe.
Otherwise, *NEVER!*"

From the mist below:
Walkie-talkie beeps, chatter.
Planning something big.

"As you like," he shouts,
"But you better get ready
For a bad hair day!"

She lets go a laugh.
Her heart slows. Her fear fizzles.
But wait . . . Listen . . . Look!

The thick mist lifts.
A blood-red chopper too, aiming
Straight for the girl's tree.

thump-thump-Thump-Thump-THUMP!
Girl and tree shake together,
Trapped in the same drum.

Wind from the chopper
Whiplashes treetop branches,
Blows up eagle's nest.

Sienna clamps on,
Arms and legs burning, screams drowned,
Retching from the fumes.

She frees up one arm,
Struggles to whip out her phone,
Then records it all.

Before the chopper
Escapes, she uploads the crime
To the World Wide Web.

It does not take long.
Her video goes viral,
Tagged: *Old-growth nightmare.*

The video works.
No one bothers girl or tree,
At least, for a while.

Closer and closer,
A cacophony of steel
Hunts down the ancients.

Closer and closer,
A crashing and crumpling, as giants
Come a-tumbling down.

Closer and closer,
A great growling and howling,
Prowls towards our tree.

Birds blast from their nests.
Wolves, bears, and elk flee from a
Choking ring of death.

Sienna hangs on,
Digging fingernails into
Wobbling plywood walls.

The ground shivers, shakes.
Huge trees sway like blades of grass.
Sienna screams, "*No-o-o-o-o-o!*"

Creeeaaak, groan, snap, crash, BAM!
Below, above, all around,
The forest explodes.

When it's all over,
This pure land lies stripped. Skinned and
Gutted like a fish.

Death and destruction
Erase the forest like it
Never existed.

Old-growth miracles
Cut clean by men and machines
Just doing their job.

Every . . . tree . . . taken,
All but Sienna's,
The last one standing.

Once a hub of life,
Now unplugged from everything
Except the empty sky.

So all alone in
The glum-grey clear-cut, like a
Ship's mast on the moon.

A soft, sighing wind
Blows through its torn bark, stirs limbs
Limp with dust and ash.

The sun holds its breath.
The tortured ground falls still.
The underworld gags.

This magnificent
Mother. Elder. Tree of life.
Giant. World-weaver.

One thousand Earth-twirls,
One million connections, slashed
By one act of greed.

What pain could it share
If our tree broke centuries
Of perfect silence?

Plunging into pain,
Drowning in defeat, the girl
Finds a crumb of strength.

Strength enough, at least,
To open the vault of her
Crumpled heart, and weep.

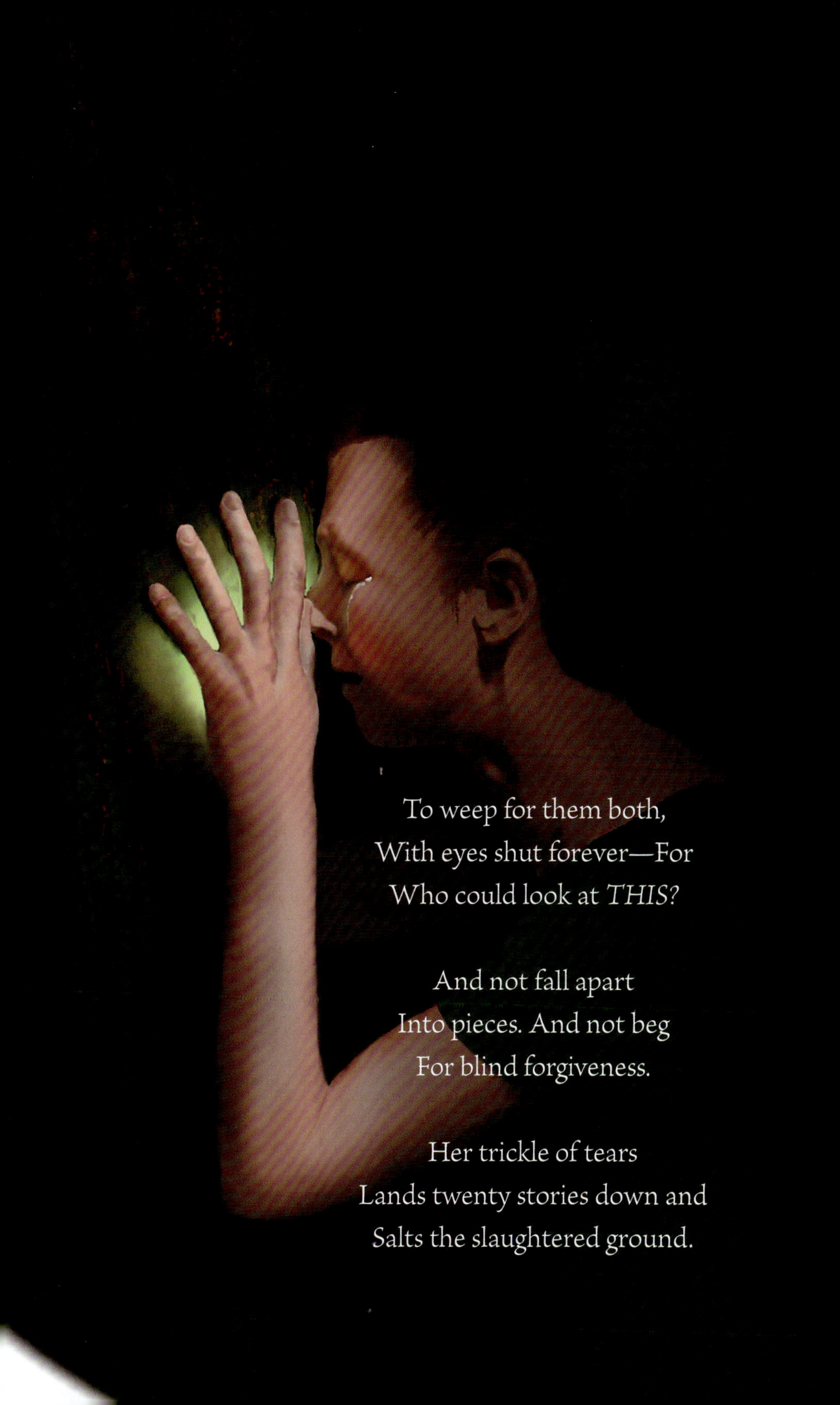

To weep for them both,
With eyes shut forever—For
Who could look at *THIS?*

And not fall apart
Into pieces. And not beg
For blind forgiveness.

Her trickle of tears
Lands twenty stories down and
Salts the slaughtered ground.

She will not look down,
But the smells waft up, in all
Their reeking glory:

Puke smoke, poisoned soil,
Burnt rubber, hydraulic oil,
The stink of squashed skunk.

She buries her face
In the tree's trunk, not knowing
Its strange bitter scent.

"I'm so, so sorry,"
Kissing sweet Mother Cedar,
"Sorry I failed you."

Freaky winds kick up
From nowhere, everywhere, fanned
By the climate crunch.

Biting rain. Clawing hail.
Steely storm. Helpless girl. "*STOP!*
We can bend no more!"

Our tree, now exposed
To every whim of the wind,
Rides a sick seesaw.

Fat moose branch fractures.
Girl's treehouse tilts, teeters, starts
To slip-slide Earthward.

Cold truth crashes in:
After seven hundred days
It's descend or die!

Nothing to do but
Grab the wind-worn rope and jump.
One big breath . . . She's gone!

Cold unblinking moon
Fixed on Big Lonely Mother,
Now just a shadow.

Battered and alone,
Our tree's bony limbs creak when
The First People come.

Sienna joins them,
With laced arms and lifted heads,
Circling Colossus.

Cedar remembers
What she can give, even now:
Healing and new life.

The night air fizzes,
Her bark buzzes, sap sizzles,
Her old branches jump!

Then . . .

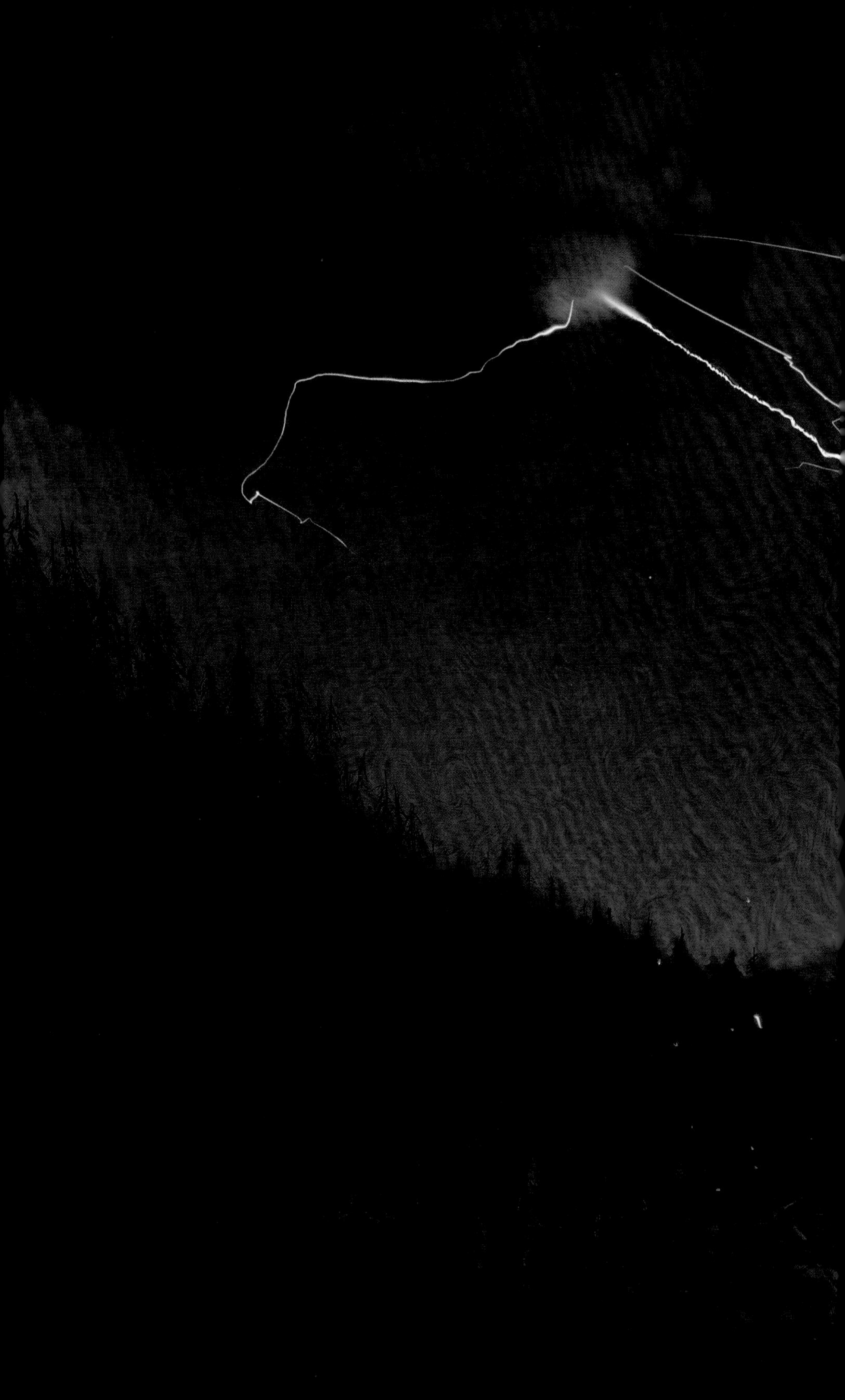

Even as she dies,
Exhaling centuries of
Creation, she gives.

Like Spring sap, life seeps
From flayed bark to fresh shoots. Oh,
The trees they can be!

I am Sienna
Old-growth forest defender.
I had to do this.

You think I'm crazy?
No. You ask, was it worth it?
Yes. Absolutely!

Clasped in her arms, she
Let me touch her deepest wounds,
Feel her sweetest joys.

She showed me the script,
Stitched on her storied body
Across deep tree-time.

Standing solid and
Strong, yet always moving, she
Let me dance with her.

In turn, I shouted,
“Please, world, save this treasured tree!”
I beat my drum for her.

Over two tough years,
We faced fierce storms together,
Shared breaths together.

Ear to her heartwood,
I learned her secret story.
Now you know it too.

The world heard our cries.
We saved one giant. The rest
Got terribly trashed.

Naked and alone,
She gave herself to the sky
And fell to its fire.

But . . .

Fallen and breathless,
She still gives life, love, and hope
To these little ones,

And, to little me,
As only a mother can.
How do I thank her?

I tell this story.

Now, as I lie on
Her perfect, broken body,
We steep in stillness,

Both embraced by the
Perennial perfume of
Decay and rebirth.

RCMP

Key References

Old-growth Forests

British Columbia is home to some of the planet's most spectacular and ancient old-growth forests. But what exactly does old-growth mean? To the BC government, it's all about the *age* of trees, so that a site clearcut and replanted many years ago could qualify if old enough. Beyond great age, more widely shared conceptions of old-growth forests include a multi-layered canopy, a diverse mix of tree species, ages, and sizes, and a rich understory which, as our story reveals, *"pulses with plush, lush life,"* both above and below ground. Long coveted by logging companies for their wealth of wood, such forests have been reduced to small pockets across BC. Only by swiftly implementing the best of government and corporate intentions to protect such forests will we save what's left.

- *Nature's Temples: A Natural History of Old-Growth Forests,* by Joan Maloof

- *Big Lonely Doug: The Story of One of Canada's Last Great Trees,* by Harley Rustad
- *Tracking Giants: Big Trees, Tiny Triumphs, and Misadventures in the Forest,* by Amanda Lewis
- *Legacy of Luna: The Story of a Tree, a Woman and the Struggle to Save the Redwoods,* by Julia Butterfly Hill
- *BC's Old Growth Forest: A Last Stand for Biodiversity,* by Karen Price, Rachel Holt, and Dave Daust
- *A New Future for Old Forests,* by Province of British Columbia

Mother Trees

Coined by Canadian forest ecologist Suzanne Simard, a "mother tree" describes large, old trees that act as communication hubs in the "wood wide web," a below-ground network of roots and fungi that allows trees to share carbon, nutrients, water, plus chemical and electrical signals with each other. This concept emphasizes the breathtaking interconnectedness and cooperation within forests, challenging traditional views of trees as solitary competitors, and is crucial to understanding what's best for forest health and wise management. Although some trees may have both male and female cones, the term

Slated for logging in the 1990s to make way for planting commercial tree species, this thousand-year-old Western Red Cedar is now protected in the Ancient Forest / Chun T'oh Whudujut Park, located 115 kilometres east of Prince George, British Columbia, on the traditional territory of the Lheidli T'enneh Indigenous people. (Photo by James Savage)

"mother tree" was chosen to spotlight the huge nurturing role these trees play in forest ecology, especially in supporting younger trees.

- *Finding the Mother Tree: Discovering the Wisdom of the Forest,* by Suzanne Simard
- *The Hidden Life of Trees: What They Feel, How They Communicate,* by Peter Wohlleben
- *To Speak for the Trees: My Life's Journey from Ancient Celtic Wisdom to a Healing Vision of the Forest,* by Diana Beresford-Kroeger
- *Entangled Life: How Fungi Make Our Worlds, Change Our Minds & Shape Our Futures,* by Merlin Sheldrake

Indigenous Connections to Cedar Trees

In this story, one ancient Western Red Cedar serves as a living bridge across deep time, embodying major events that shape it—"*Imprints of moose, snow . . . gashes and gifts from humans . . .*" Over the span of a millennium, a huge proportion of the human interactions with this tree inevitably would be with Indigenous forest-dwellers. This species' status as British Columbia's official tree honours its immeasurable importance to Indigenous people for traditional construction, transportation, tools, clothing, medicine, and ceremonial artifacts. While such cultural connections continue to thrive, their historic expression can also be read in "culturally modified trees," which bear vivid evidence of careful harvesting procedures that protected the tree and speak to the centuries-long intimacy of this unique human-tree relationship.

- *The Geography of Memory: Reclaiming the Cultural, Natural and Spiritual History of the Snayackstx (Sinixt) First People,* by Eileen Delehanty Pearkes
- *Cedar: Tree of Life to the Northwest Coast Indians,* by Hilary Stewart
- *Culturally Modified Trees of British Columbia: A Handbook for the Identification and Recording of Culturally Modified Trees,* by Province of British Columbia
- *Braiding Sweetgrass: Indigenous Wisdom, Scientific Knowledge and the Teachings of Plants,* by Robin Wall Kimmerer
- *The Songs of Trees: Stories from Nature's Great Connectors,* by David Haskell
- *Worth More Standing: Poets and Activists Pay Homage to Trees,* Edited by Christine Lowther

Acknowledgments

Four books had a massive influence on the spirit and substance of this story. It started with forest ecologist Suzanne Simard's *Finding the Mother Tree: Discovering the Wisdom of the Forest,* which documents the astounding connections and support systems spilling from veteran trees in a healthy forest. Thank you Suzanne for articulating the "Mother Tree" concept and helping science catch up with truths long-held by forest-based cultures around the world. I trust that we have honoured this concept in our book.

I next reached for a copy of *Big Lonely Doug: The Story of One of Canada's Last Great Trees,* by investigative journalist Harley Rustad. This gripping book stirs together currents on old-growth forests, the state of British Columbia's logging industry, forest preservation battles, and First Nation land rights, all swirling around one giant Douglas Fir tree that was spared while everything around it was cut and carted away. What a timely tale well told! Thank you, Harley.

This book led me to an amazing story of another colossal tree and one woman's heroic efforts to protect it, *Legacy of Luna: The Story of a Tree, a Woman, and the Struggle to Save the Redwoods,* by Julia Lorraine (Butterfly) Hill. Thank you, Julia, for writing your jaw-dropping story and for the inspiration it gave me to create the young heroine, Sienna, in my own.

A Nelson friend, Stuart McKinnon, familiar with my "tree book" project, one day insisted I join him at a talk by Eileen Delehanty Pearkes about her book, *The Geography of Memory: Reclaiming the Cultural, Natural and Spiritual History of the Snayackstx (Sinixt) First People.* Eileen's book impressed upon me the value—and, ultimately, the *necessity*—of weaving together natural, cultural, and spiritual threads in any story about the land, including this one, and for this inspiration I am very grateful.

As this story took shape and I began writing in earnest, image after image sprang to mind, and I knew that this book cried out for an illustrator. I shared this insight with a dear friend, Jim Savage, who, besides being the Best Man at my wedding, and a fellow adventurer in the Yukon wilds, is a highly accomplished artist. "Why not throw your name in the hat?" I challenged Jim, when my publisher, Fitzhenry & Whiteside, asked me to recommend an illustrator. And so it came to pass that the then-chief operating officer, Holly Doll, said *yes*, and Jim and I began a precious partnership that deepened both our understanding of this story and our friendship of over forty-five years. Thanks for that thumbs-up, Holly, and Jim, for your numinous, luminous art!

Once Jim came on board, we waded deeper into our story, together discovering new depths and directions. The need for cultural engagement soon came into sharp focus once we realized that, among the countless humans to touch the life of this ancient tree, the lion's share of them would be Indigenous people. But, having learned from *The Geography of Memory* about the pitfalls of pan-indigenization—a problematic "one-size-fits-all" approach that erases unique cultural and political differences among First Nations—the question became, *Which* Indigenous people?

The natural range of this book's featured species, the Western Red Cedar, encompasses many distinct First Nations, both in Canada and the United States, each with their own unique ways of using and honouring this treasured tree. I concluded that, what better place to situate our tree than in the bioregion where I lived while writing this book, the Upper Columbian Mountains of south-central British Columbia and north-eastern Washington state, best represented by the Sinixt First People, the focus of Eileen's book.

But from the outset, we knew that it would be culturally inappropriate for us to represent the Sinixt people in any way without seeking their acceptance and genuine involvement in the project. It was only after engaging with Sinixt educator, Stevey Seymour, of the Inchelium Language & Culture Association in Colville, Washington, that we were blessed to receive the kind of fine-toothed scrutiny of the draft book that we needed to assure its cultural authenticity. Thank you so much Stevey for your guidance! We are also very grateful to Stevey's mother, Shelly Boyd, her colleague Herb Alex in Nelson's Sinixt office, cultural bridge-builder Allison Girvan, and wise advisor Pamela Millar, all of whom helped us cultivate this essential alliance.

With Stevey Seymour's help, Jim and I, in portraying any cultural practices of the Sinixt, took great care to convey them with a sense of empathy, respect, accuracy, and clear acknowledgement of the main character's—and the book's creators'—non-Indigenous or "settler" status. Also, only publicly available academic and Indigenous source materials were used to enhance the credibility of such practices in the story. We took these steps to portray all Indigenous interactions with this tree as realistically and respectfully as possible, applying the same careful standards to both the poetry and the artwork.

Still, for any cultural misrepresentations that might have slipped through our research and review process, Jim and I shoulder full responsibility.

For hugely helpful feedback on the draft manuscript, we thank poets Rayya Liebich and Sonnet L'Abbé, biologist John Theberge, authors Ross Breithaupt and Hayden Trenholm, and musician Stuart McKinnon. For bringing an artist's eye to the draft illustrations, we thank Pamela Millar, Allison Girvan, and Cathie Allen. And for serving as models for several illustrations, a huge thanks—*mahsi cho!*—to Brad Thom, Nimisha and Jaya Bastedo, Brenda Hans, Matt Biehn, Mindy Willet, Damian Panayi, Mike Savage, Rob Borsato, plus a small cast of keen kids.

We offer deep gratitude to the project's editor, Penny Hosey, to Tanya St. Amand for initial design work, and to all the skilled staff and contractors at Sutherland House who helped shepherd this work to bookshelves around the world: Kenneth Whyte, Shalomi Ranasinghe, Kimberlene Francis, and Karl Hunt.

Finally, a glowing thanks to my wife, Brenda for, once again, supporting my writing habit with freshly baked cookies, bouquets on my desk, and boots out the door to recharge my batteries on some wild mountain trail . . .

Jamie Bastedo, October 2025
Smithers, British Columbia

Other Books by Jamie Bastedo

Children

- *Free as the Wind: Saving the Wild Horses of Sable Island*
- *Nighthawk!*

Teens

- *Tracking Triple Seven*
- *On Thin Ice*
- *Sila's Revenge*
- *The Horrors: Terrifying Tales, Book Two* (edited by Peter Carver)
- *Protectors of the Planet: Environmental Trailblazers from 7 to 97*

Adult

- *Shield Country: The Life and Times of the Oldest Piece of the Planet*
- *Reaching North: A Celebration of the Subarctic*
- *Falling for Snow: A Naturalist's Journey into the World of Winter*
- *ABC Resource Survey Method for Environmentally Significant Areas*
- *Northwest Territories: Trans Canada Trail Official Guide*
- *Blue Lake and Rocky Shore: A Field Guide to Special Natural Areas in the Yellowknife Region*

About the Author

Jamie Bastedo's works create a sparkling tapestry of stories drawn from his skills as a biologist, educator, broadcaster, entertainer, and writer. He has authored fourteen books and over 100 articles on a vast array of nature topics, from Canada's basement bedrock to its shimmering northern lights. Jamie's latest novel, *Cut Off*, about a cyber-addict "screenager" who finds deliverance on a wild northern river, earned a *Kirkus* starred review. His recent nonfiction, *Protectors of the Planet*, shines a spotlight on some of Canada's best and brightest environmental trailblazers, described by *CM Magazine* as "an informative and entertaining read that should spur even the most apathetic to action." Among Jamie's many awards are the *Michael Smith Award for Science Promotion, Rustrum Wilderness Trust Author's Award, White Ravens International Youth Library Selection of Outstanding Books*, and a *Queen Elizabeth's Golden Jubilee Medal*. Formerly from Yellowknife, Jamie now lives in a lively co-housing community in Smithers, BC. (www.fitzhenry.ca/jamie-bastedo)

About the Illustrator

James Savage's contemporary realism is inspired by deep experience of rural life and wild nature. He is an artist, musician, and community economic development worker who was raised and lives in a forestry-dependent town in British Columbia. Further to this lovely story, he understands the economic importance of the forest industry, as well as the ecologically unsustainable nature of much of the industry as currently practiced.

Jim is honoured to have his art in homes in Canada, the US, the UK, and Europe. Learn more at savageart.ca.

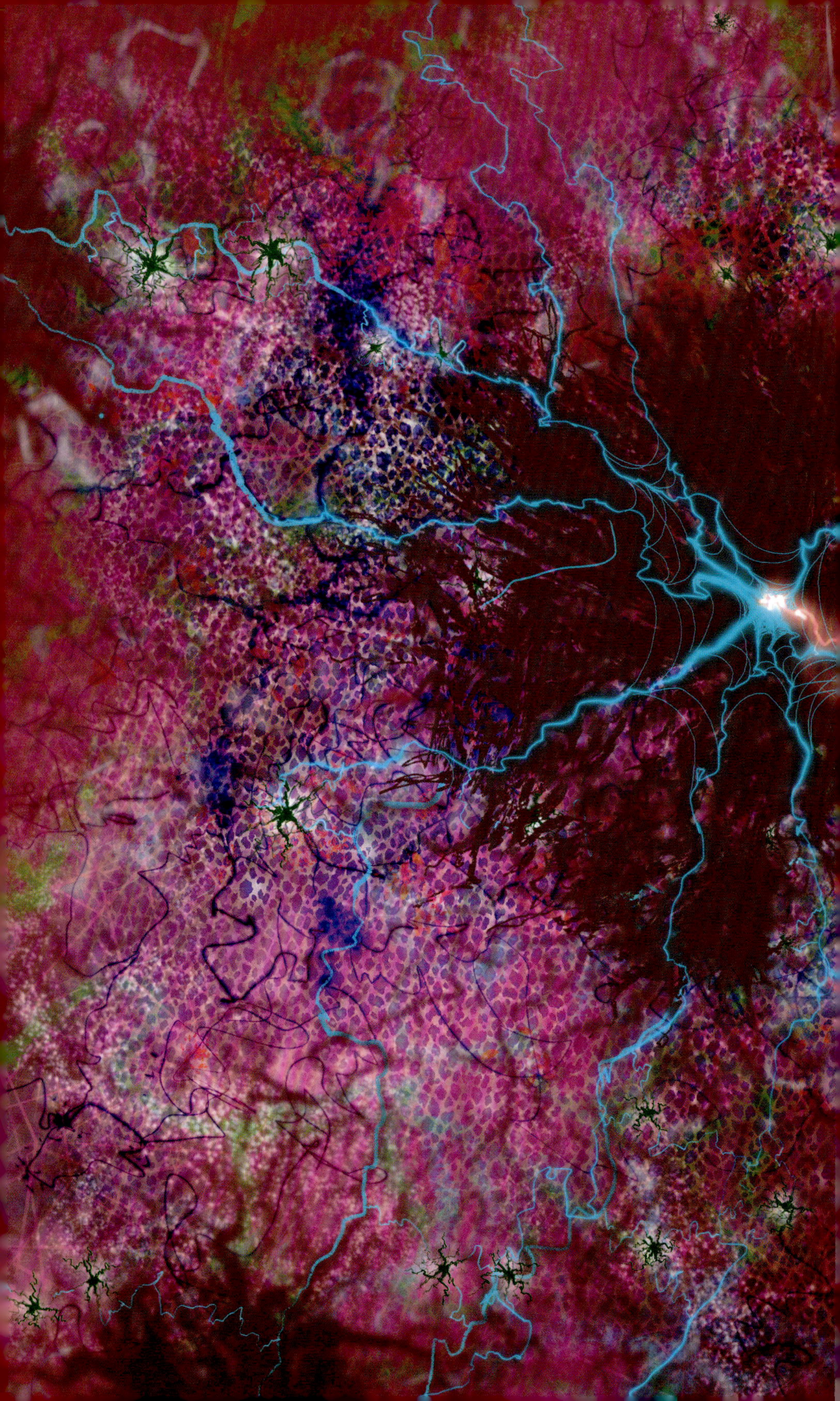

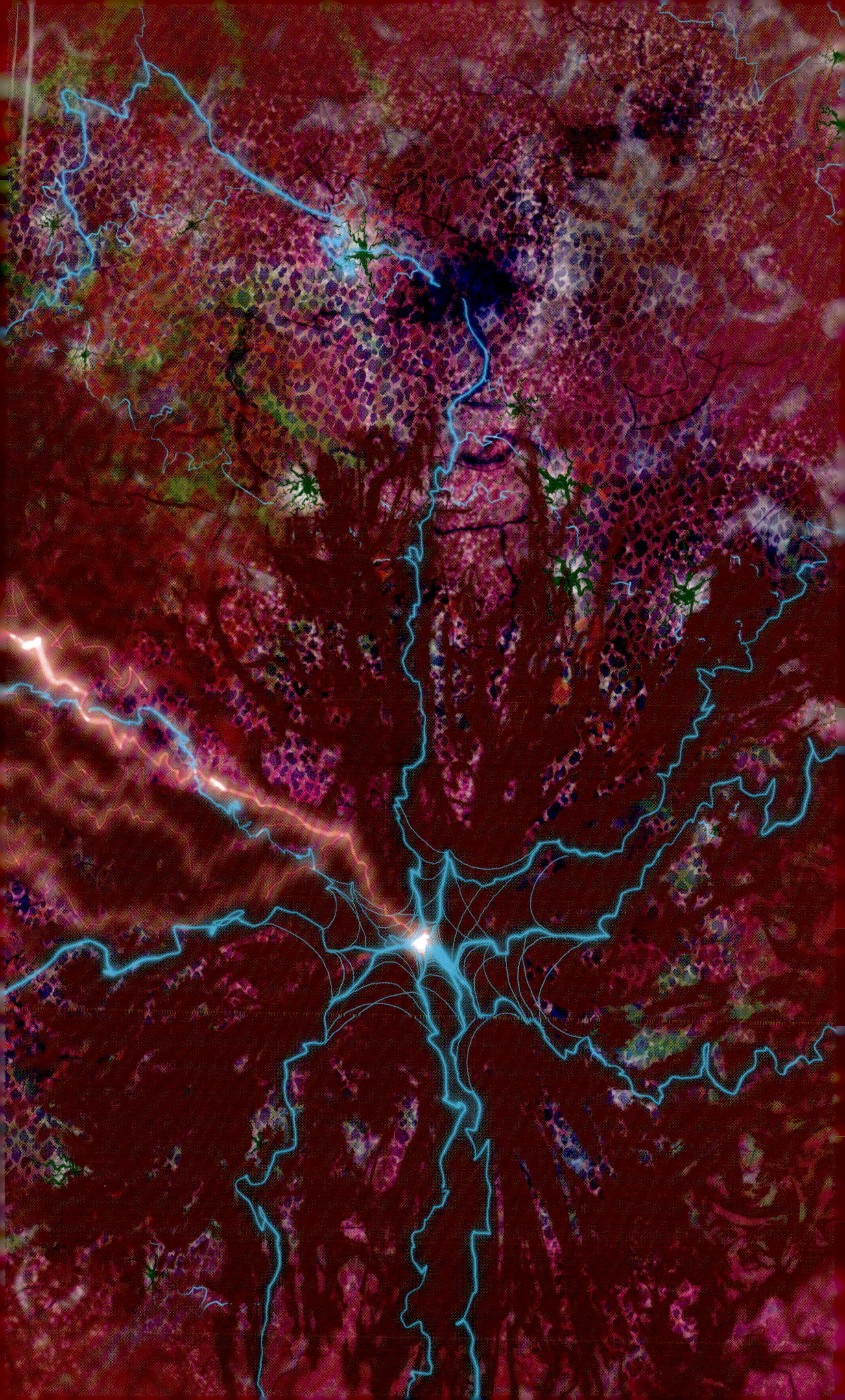